Chicken Coops for Beginners:

Find Answers On Any Questions You Have Planning Your Perfect Chicken Coops!

Table of content

Introduction

I would like to thank and congratulate you on downloading *'Chicken Coops for Beginners: Find Answers on Any Questions You Have Planning Your Own Perfect Chicken Coops!'* Just think how wonderful it will be for you and your loved ones to have your own fresh organic eggs, that your own chickens supplied you with! You will be so glad that you made the decision to start raising your own chickens, especially with the rising costs of foods and the added chemicals in foods sold in the markets. You can feel at ease when you are eating your eggs, because you will know that they were not exposed to any harmful chemicals.

Deciding to raise your own chickens will be a source of food for you and your loved ones for years. Just think of all the delicious chicken meat dishes and egg dishes you can create using your own chickens and eggs. If you are wondering "what comes first the chicken or the chicken coop?" Well I can tell you it is the chicken coop. So, before you can begin to raise your own chickens you are going to need a chicken coop to house them in. Follow the tips and suggestions in this book to help get you started in creating them.

Chapter 1. Learning How to Understand Chickens

Now before we get into the construction of your chicken coops, that will be their haven, I want to begin with an education chapter. In this chapter I want to focus on talking to you about chickens, what you will need to do to care for and maintain your chickens. In the following chapter, we will then explore how you can create the chicken coops that will be the perfect home for your chickens.

This is an important chapter, that you really should not skip over. Many people may feel that they have enough knowledge about chickens already, and are just looking for a way to build a good chicken coop. Well if this is you then go ahead and jump to the next chapter, but I would suggest that you read this chapter anyway even if it is just to give yourself a refresher on your knowledge of chickens.

People who have chickens often wish that they had known more about chickens before they had got them. Below is a list that I hope will be helpful to you.

Question #1. What size should I make my chicken coop?
This is a common question and it is one that you should take a lot of thought on answering. When we begin raising chickens, many of us have no idea how much fun and how addictive they can be. We are also unaware of just how much space and maintenance they require. Based on this reason many people make the mistake of making their chicken coops far too small, this results in diminishing their capacity to care and grow their chicken stock.

The wise rule of thumb is to plan for three times as many chickens that you want to have. This way you will have room to expand and incorporate additional chickens and you can be more aware if you are growing too fast.

Question #2. Do chickens get sick?
Yes, your chickens can get sick, as they are living creatures and susceptible to a lot of illnesses. You can do research on common chicken illnesses and learn what the treatments are. You will want to learn all there is to know about chickens so that you can ensure your chickens are in good health.

Question #3. Are chickens smart and do they have their own personalities?
Yes. Chickens are very intelligent animals, they have thoughts and emotions. When you study your chickens, you will soon pick up on their individual mannerisms and specific traits. View how they interact with one another. Once you spend some time observing them you will soon figure out who rules the roost.

Question #4. Are Chickens Fun to Have?
Chicken owners quickly realize just how fun raising chickens can be. Often as a result they want to more and more of them. People often find themselves becoming very attached to their chickens. You might want to go to a chicken ranch to get the feel of what raising chickens can be like. It can help you to decide if raising chickens is something you can see yourself doing.

Question #5. How domesticated are chickens?
The modern chicken is a very domesticated animal. Many people feel that because of this they need a lot of tending to. However, the truth is that chickens

can pretty much take care of themselves. All you need to do is to supply them with some basic food, water and shelter, they can fend for themselves. Make sure to keep their cages clean and your chickens should live long and healthy lives.

Question #6. What about other animals?

People often wonder how other animals will react to their chickens. It will depend on what types of animals you have in your area. Some problems that other people have noticed raising chickens was an increase in rodent problems. I am not sure whether this is due to the odor or that the food is available in the open. Many people find that they get a lot of unwanted guests.

Larger predatory animals may also become an issue. These animals will look at your chickens as a source of food for them. You will need to take extra precautions to ensure the safety of your chickens.

Question #7. Do I need any kind of special chicken litter?

There are diverse ways of dealing with cleaning up after your chickens. Some people like to use some form of composting, some use straw, others use dead leaves and some use sand. When using sand, it is easy to clean, and chickens seem to love it. You may want to experiment with a few types of materials and see which one works best for you.

Question #8. Rooster or not rooster?

Many people wonder if they should have a rooster in the pen with their hens. The answer is a personal choice as well as a legal one. First, on the legal side. You will need to know if your ordinances and state codes allow you to have roosters. There are areas where roosters are a public nuisance.

The next thing that you want to consider is if you want to have baby chicks. A standard female chicken can lay an egg without the assistance of a rooster. A rooster is only needed if you want to have eggs that will grow into chicks to repopulate your stock.

Once a chicken becomes impregnated by the rooster you can no longer eat the egg. If you do it is going to taste fowl and depending on the development of the chicken it would be unwise to try and eat it.

Question #9. Should I use chicken wire?

Most people when they decide to build a chicken coop naturally think they will need some chicken wire to keep in their chickens. Well this is good to help keep the chicken in, but what will you do to keep the predators out? Many people choose to use a hardwire cloth.

Hardwire cloth is a very fine mesh of wire cloth that has small holes in it compared to chicken wire that has larger holes. If you use chicken wire small rodents such as mice and rats can squeeze through and get the food.

Larger animals such as opossums, raccoons and larger predators will use the chicken wire to climb up, and chew through it or just grab hold of the wire and make their way through it.

When using hardware cloth, it will make the surface of the chicken coop less penetrable by outside attack. It is also much harder to climb so it will help to deter creatures from trying to get on top of your chicken coops.

Question #10. How much do chickens poop?

This is a question that many people ask when they are deciding whether to raise their own chickens or not. Chickens do poop a lot.

Question #11. Where do I go if my chickens become sick?

If your chickens become sick, you will either need to have the medical knowledge to care for them or you will need to know where a local vet is that specializes in the care of chickens.

These are the top questions that most people are interested in knowing about. You can go online and look for forums or on Facebook groups that talk about this topic and locate an expert.

Now that we have a better understanding about chickens, it is now time to move forward to the next chapter and start considering creating chicken coops and what you will need to design your own great chicken coop.

Chapter 2. Building Your Perfect Chicken Coop

So, you are ready to build your own chicken coop? I can imagine that your mind is racing wondering what and how you are going to create your chicken coop.

The first thing you should realize is that chicken coops do not have to look ugly or stick out like a sore thumb. When it comes to chicken coops, we want to have some basic functionality inside of the coop and a container area on the outside of it, and the rest of the coop can be your own personal style and preferences.

When it comes to building chick coops, all they need is protection from predators, a roost that they can sit on and sleep, nesting boxes to lay their eggs and plenty of room for them to run around in.

You will need an area where you can supply them with food and water. You will also want easy access to be able to clean the coops when needed. Other than that, you will have full control over the design and look of your coops.

Now let us not get too ahead of ourselves, let us do a little prep work first. The first thing that you should check is that the area you are living in is zoned to support chickens. You want to take steps to ensure that your investment is going to be safe. Once you have the okay to have chickens, the next step is to seek out a spot on your property that will best suit your chickens. Find a location that is away from the house and yet has easy access. Look to see if you have any natural shelter that can be of benefit to your chickens such as large trees and a natural water source and large hedges.

You need to consider the general maintenance as well. You do not want to place your coop too close to a tree or create a blocked off area in your yard that you are unable to get to with a lawnmower or other equipment.

Take the time needed, to plan your coop location. Go through the pros and cons of various locations on your property, until you settle on the best location. You should have several different access points to your coop. The first access point should be where you can clean the coop easily.

Many people create a door in the back of their chicken coop as a door. How you do this is you unlatch the back of the coop and open it like a door. Then you will have easy access to your entire chicken coop. You can clean out the coop and make sure that your chickens are as comfortable as possible.

The next thing you are going to want to consider is your access to the egg laying area. When you are designing your coop, you will want to make this area dark and a comfortable spot for your chickens. Chickens like to lay their eggs in private, so make sure that you create an environment that is conducive to this but at the same time you will have easy access to.

Food and Water

Food and water is another item that you will need to pay close attention to. You are going to want to have a system setup that will easily load up your chicken's food and water dishes on a regular basis without having to enter the coop each time. You can develop a shoot system to accomplish this. Using a series of PBP pipes that are about an inch and a half in diameter you can cap off at one end when not in use. The pipe is angled at a 45-degree angle which allows a steady flow of food and water for your chickens.

This pipe will be located on the top tier of the feed tray. The feed will naturally spill out into the tray allowing the chickens to gain access to the new food. You will have another pipe that you will fill with water setup the same way.

This can help to make cleaning your coops easier as well as staying out of the way of your chickens while they are running around tending to their chicken business.

Doll House or Shed Look

The first style of chicken coop you may decide to build is the doll house or shed. When you are designing your chicken coop you may want to think of your chickens as little people. You will want to have a door, windows, shingles and a roof and a wheel chair ramp going up the front of it.

In the yard, you can create their screened in area to have a picket fence or screened-in porch. You can add hanging plants and even paint the coop a tropical color to blend in with the property, when people look at it they will not even realize there is chickens in there because it blends in with the property.

Apartment Building

This design is good if you are having a set number of chickens in your coop. You can build a three-story structure. On the first level, you can have the egg laying area. On the second and third levels, you can have roosting areas for your chickens. You will have a walkway going up into the coop that will allow your chickens to get in and out of the coop. Build an outside roaming area for your chickens either at the side of the coop or in the front.

Brooding Cabinet

These are not a full chicken coop, but you can build these to add-on buildings for your chickens to lay their eggs in. How this works is you take an old cabinet or piece of tall furniture you have laying around.

You could design it in such a way that the front would be a screen door that you could open to place the chickens into the nesting boxes. Once they have laid their eggs you could allow them to roam free by removing them or placing them into your main coop. This is a clever idea if you want to breed specific chickens and keep them away from the general population.

Log Cabin or Barn

This is another fun great look for your coops. You can make your coop look like an old-fashioned barn or like a cute rustic log cabin. You could get creative and add deer heads to the cabin. You can incorporate the entire structure in one building so that your chickens are not exposed to the elements, except when they decide to go outside.

Repurpose a swing set or other items

A good thing to do is to repurpose old things that you have lying around the house. One thing that many of us have had in our yards at one time or another is a swing set. You can take your old swing set and attach your chicken wire or hardware screen to the outside of the swing. You can then build a small covered area where your chickens will be protected from the elements. Using materials such as some old aluminum slides or other flat material.

You can use old materials by repurposing them, just giving them a coat of paint can have them looking like new.

Repurpose children's outgrown toys

Do you remember those plastic houses that kids would play in for hours? When the kids have outgrown them, you can repurpose them by making them into chicken coops. You can repaint them and place them on a platform and build a running area where they are screened in with hardware wire or chicken wire.

Using old toys in this way will certainly give the neighbors something to talk about, before long they could be calling you the neighborhood mother hen.

The giant bird house

You can build a large version of a bird feeder or treehouse. You can place it on top of a large concrete pillar in your yard. You would build your chicken coop on top of the concrete pillar. You would have runners coming down from it to give your chickens easy access to it. You can enclose it in a fenced-in area with hardware cloth or chicken wire.

Use reclaimed wood

Using reclaimed wood to build chicken coops is great. You can easily use drift wood, old doors, uneven boards or anything and everything that you find lying around. You can take a trip to a construction site to see if they have any scraps of wood they have no use for. You can even visit local lumber stores where they have may have scraps of wood that you can make use of in building your chicken coop.

Re-purpose a crib

You can use an old style of baby crib to use to create your chicken coop from. Use and old wooden crib and enclose the slits with chicken wire or hardware screen and cut a hole in the front for the chickens to come in and out. Build a ramp so the chickens have easy access to it. Paint it a nice color and you have yourself a great little chicken coop made from refurbished material.

Chapter 3. Tips and Tricks for Designing Chicken Coops

In this concluding section of the book we are going to look at some tips and tricks that you can use when you are designing and constructing your chicken coops. Some of these will be general and based on common sense but others will spark something within you that could ultimately save you hours of work.

Tip #1 Take your time on your chicken coop project

Now in many cases this goes without saying. The truth of the matter is many people will view the project as just a chicken coop and will try to bypass some of the critical details that are important.

It is important to slow down, take your time and really build yourself a multi-purpose structure. When you have this in mind you are going to create a building that is a functional structure and not a "Chicken Coop."

Tip #2 Consider purchasing a chick coop kit or plans

Most of you will be new to building chicken coops, this is probably the first one you have built. There may be some of you reading this book that are thinking it will be a very easy project to accomplish. Chicken coops are not considered to be complicated projects, but there are some fine points that need to be addressed. If you purchase a chicken coop kit or plans, it will make your first chicken coop experience much easier.

Tip #3 Keep your chicken coop build simple

You should focus first on strength and security. You want to create a structure that is going to be safe for your chickens, which means taking steps to ensure that predators will not be able to get in. You do not have to create Fort Knox, but you need to ensure that you have padlocks on your doors, do not use sliding latches—lock them up.

Invest in strong screens so that animals cannot easily cut their way into your coop. You want to create a coop where you have easy access but others do not.

Tip #4 Try using recycled material for your coop project

Use recycled material whenever you can. Keep in mind that you are creating a chicken coop not a play house for your kids. It needs to be a functional structure for your chickens. It will be covered in chicken poop in no time, so do not purchase the best wood in the world. Use reclaimed wood or anything that you have laying around. The more recycled materials you use in your chicken coop project the more you will cut down on overall costs for the project.

Tip #5 Be very detailed if you have decided to create your own plans

If you have your heart set on creating a custom coop it is highly suggested that you make plans as detailed as possible. You are going to want to know exactly what you need and want right down to the last nail and piece of wood.

When it comes to you creating your coop you can take some liberties and adjust to specific situations but as long as you have your plans written down there shouldn't be any surprises.

Tip #6 Roosting is top priority

Chickens love to roost. So, it is important that you construct some suitable roosting areas for your chickens. When you are designing your coop focus on the roosting areas of your coop. The more room that your chickens to roost the happier and more productive they will be.

Tip #7 Size your coops to accommodate your chickens

Chickens love space, so you need to be able to give this to them. You will want to have three to six square feet of living space per chicken. Depending on the space you must work with, you may want to consider building up instead of out. The environment that your chickens will be living in is also a major factor to consider.

Tip #8 Moveable or stationary coop

You may want to consider making a movable coop. The advantage to the movable coop is that they are small and lightweight. With the movable coop, you can move your chickens to different areas. This can be great if you want to locate the coop closer to your house during the winter months for example. You can then incorporate a heat source for your chickens from interior power as well to do maintenance on that area of the yard that is surviving the punishment of your chickens.

Of course, the decision will be left up to you, but they both have their advantages and disadvantages. It will be well worth your while to research diverse types of coops to find one that will best suit your needs.

Tip #9 Nice and Cozy Nesting Boxes

A nesting box may not look very inviting to you, but they certainly will appeal to your chickens. You want to design nesting boxes that your chickens will love.

When there is enough room in the box for some bedding material and room for them to move around, they will be in there getting comfortable and getting down to the business of laying eggs. If they really like their nesting boxes they will stay in them longer and will produce more eggs for you than you can eat.

Tip #10 Build a coop that suits you and your chickens

The chicken coop that you decide to build will have to suit your needs and your chickens. This means that for you having easy access to the coop will be a crucial factor in deciding what design of coop to choose. Your chickens will need comfort and security which you can provide by constructing a safe and secure home for them. If you keep this in mind while you are building your chicken coop I am sure it will be a very enjoyable experience for you.

Tip #11 Work on the functional details first

When creating your chicken coop make sure to work out all of your functional details first. Make sure that your chickens are going to be secure and comfortable in the design you are choosing. When your chickens are happy they will produce eggs in abundance. So, keep this in mind when you are designing your chicken coop. Make it easy for you to access while at the same time create a comfortable home for chickens.

Tip #12 Start out small

I would suggest that you start out small. I would not get no more than five chickens to start with. Study your chickens and learn their behaviors and needs. Once you do this and become more comfortable with raising chickens, then you can always expand.

Tip #13 Care for your chickens

Many people that raise chickens see it as a labor of love. Often people become very attached to their chickens and are saddened when they pass. Remember why you got chickens in the first place. Take care of your chickens and they in turn will take care of you.

Tip #14 Collect old egg cartons

Start collecting your old egg cartons, so when you start raising chickens you will have some egg cartons to store your eggs in. This is just a simple step in your planning ahead and preparing for the day you will have your own egg supply. You might get to a point where you will begin to sell your excess of eggs.

Tip #15 Easiest ways to clean, feed, water and collect eggs

It is important that you really think long and hard on the best kind of design will be for a chicken coop. You want to make a chicken coop that is going to make it easy for you to clean the coop, feed, water and collect the eggs.

You do not want to make a chicken coop that might look cute, but it does not function well, as it is a design that makes it awkward for you to access the coop to clean it for example.

Chapter 4. Chicken Coop Plans for Beginners

In this chapter I have included three effective chicken coops that will suit the needs of a beginner chicken raiser.

PVC Chicken Coop

This chicken coop design might be the simplest chicken coop design out there. To put this coop together you will be emulating the shape of a high tunnel or classic hoop house. This design is also perfect for those who are working with a small budget. You can use pre-bent plastic hoops to the make the construction a lot easier. When it rains or snows, you can place a tarp over the coop to shelter your chickens from the weather.

Instructions:

Step 1: Create the frames. Make sure that you bend one pipe first to see how high you would like the coop to be. The height will define how long you will want the frame to be.

Step 2: Once you have decided on the size of coop you want, bend the other pipes and attach them to the frame you create. For this design, there was 6 pipes bent. Have a person to help you with securing the screw. Make sure that the bent pipes are at least a foot apart.

Step 3: Cover your foundations with mesh wire and use zip ties in order to secure the mesh wire to your pipes.

Step 4: To create the door, simply cut a PVC pipe into pieces to the size you want, ideally 2x2 feet. Attach them together, making a square frame and cover it with mesh wire. Cut the mesh of the coop area where you intend the door to be, and again secure with zip ties.

Pyramid Chicken Coop

This coop is popular with many chicken owners simply because they like the look of it. This will require some construction skills to build because it has precise edges and angles.

A pyramid chicken coop has an access at one side of the roof which is where the eggs are being collected. It is a superior design for limited space, it works well with one or two chickens or a hen with her chicks.

Instructions

Step 1: Choose an area where it is slightly elevated so that water can run-off when it rains.

Step 2: Once you have chosen the size of your coop, go ahead and pre-cut the wood for your specifications. Ideally you should be using 4 pieces of your chosen material attached by screws to create the floor. At all corners, lean the pre-cut sides at 45-degree angle; this makes an A-frame. Each side must have a length of about 3 feet or proportional to the base.

Step 3: Attach the A-frame together with the screws.

Step 4: Cover the whole exterior with mesh wire, except for the back of the chicken coop. Secure it with fencing fasteners.

Step 5: For the interior of the chicken coop, repeat the process of the exterior. Except for the mesh wire, use plywood for a complete cover. Don't forget to make a door access on the back of the coop.

Dog House Mini Chicken Coop

This is a low-cost chicken coop design. It is perfect for those who are building a chicken coop for the first time, as it does not require a lot of construction. It is also portable and when it is done correctly, it will protect your chickens.

This, however, does require a doghouse. So, if you have a dog house that is not being used, this would be a perfect choice for you in a chicken coop design.

Instructions

Step 1: Cut 1x2-inch mesh fencing and make the sides of the pen 3x10-foot.

Step 2: Cut an 11-ft length of the 2x4-inch mesh wire, bend 6 inches below on both ends to have a piece that is 10-ft long. Using hog rings every 4-6 inches, put the 2x4-inch wire together to make your top for the 3x10-foot wire in a rectangular shape.

Step 3: Create another 10-foot piece, flip it over and attach the next section.

Step 4: When you are creating your access for your coop, make a 1 to 1 end so that it will be easier for you to clean the house and collect the eggs from the nest—cut parts of the wire out of every end of the pen to create openings that are wide and tall enough for the doghouse to easily slide in and out. Make sure to bend all the sharp pieces of wire to avoid injuries.

Step 5: When you are creating the doors, make two 3x1 1/2 -foot flaps of the 1x2-inch mesh fencing that flips from the bottom up; the bottom and top flaps are going to overlay 6 inches in the center. This kind of door will allow you to open just the top flap when you need to collect the eggs. You can use bungee cords to make sure that the door will not open on its own.

Step 6: File off the tabs that attach the roof to the bottom, when you are attaching the dog house. This will make it easier for you when you need to take the roof off to change the bedding. Then attach a 1x2-inch board to stand as the roost over the edge of the bottom, and install thin plywood as a crosspiece to the back of the coop, drill a hole so the hens can lay eggs somewhere private. Place the roof of the doghouse backwards so that you have a bigger opening in the front when you must retrieve the eggs, and have a smaller opening at the back, just enough for the chickens to access the mesh walls.

Conclusion

Well hopefully my tips and suggestions on how to get yourself started on a project of building a chicken coop will help things go easier for you. Basically, when it comes to designing chicken coops the sky is the limit. As you can see just from the suggestions in this book, there is so many varied materials and items that you can re-furbish to create a wonderful chicken coop for yourself and chickens. You do not have to go into any great expense for materials to build yourself a functional chicken coop out of used materials. You just need to get the old creative juices flowing and get a pen and paper and start writing down your ideas for designing that special and unique chicken coop of yours.

In this book, we considered some of the fundamental questions answered you can then stub those out in your plans and build your coop around your own plans. I hope you liked some of the ideas that I have offered you regarding things to use and designs for chicken coops. I would strongly suggest that you draw out your chicken coop plans on paper before you begin the build.

I would like to thank you for downloading my book, and supporting my work, it is most appreciated. I would love to read a review of my book by you on Amazon.

FREE Bonus Reminder

If you have not grabbed it yet, please go ahead and download your special bonus report *"DIY Projects. 13 Useful & Easy To Make DIY Projects To Save Money & Improve Your Home!"*

Simply Click the Button Below

OR **Go to This Page**

http://diyhomecraft.com/free

BONUS #2: More Free & Discounted Books or Products

Do you want to receive more Free/Discounted Books or Products?

We have a mailing list where we send out our new Books or Products when they go free or with a discount on Amazon. Click on the link below to sign up for Free & Discount Book & Product Promotions.

=> Sign Up for Free & Discount Book & Product Promotions <=

OR Go to this URL

http://zbit.ly/1WBb1Ek

www.ingramcontent.com/pod-product-compliance
Lightning Source LLC
Chambersburg PA
CBHW071321280526
45788CB00004B/1967